The Author Effect

An Easy Plan to Write a Book for Your Business
and Become an Industry Authority

*A Complete Beginner's Guide to Self-Publishing
Your First Nonfiction Book*

The Author Effect

An Easy Plan to Write a Book For Your Business and Become an Industry Authority

A Complete Beginner's Guide to Self-Publishing
Your First Nonfiction Book

by
Sandra Shillington

Table of Contents

"A professional writer is an amateur who didn't quit."

—Richard Bach

Introduction

Congratulations on getting serious about writing a book for your business. Since you're reading this book, you know the impact of becoming a published author:

- You'll stand out from your peers and become an authority in your space.
- People will know you as "the person who wrote the book on…"
- New opportunities will come your way.
- Clients will seek you out as the expert on your subject.

One of the biggest obstacles many people have when trying to write a book is they don't have a plan of action. The questions are simple, but they always get in the way: When can I find the time to write? How much should I write each day? How long should my book be? How do I edit my work? How do I get my manuscript ready? In this book I share the process I've used to write and publish five Amazon bestselling books for my own business, and you can do it too. Don't Wait! It's time to write your book and open up all the opportunities that will come as a result. You can do this even if you don't know where to start, you're not good at writing, or you're overwhelmed by the idea of writing and publishing a book. If you want to stay on top of the latest advice on designing and building courses, writing and publishing books, and creating audio, video and written assets for your business, Join my Facebook Group, Mighty Online Creators. It's for entrepreneurs, business owners and professionals who want to make a bigger impact (and more income) by creating an online course, self-publishing a book, writing a blog, starting a podcast or YouTube Channel, or launching a freelance career.

Join Mighty Online Creators at:

facebook.com/groups/MightyOnlineCreators/

You may also like **The Guided Writer Self-Publishing Course.** Based on feedback from my readers, I've learned many people like the idea of having someone to coach them through the writing and publishing process. In this action-oriented course, I guide you through the process, step-by-step, of writing and self-publishing your book from start-to finish.

Sign up for my course:

Get Published

Guided Writer
C o u r s e

guidedwritercourse.writerrs.com

You might also like my **FREE Faster Writing Cheat Sheet** that contains even more quick tips on how to write your book faster.

Get your free Cheat Sheet at fasterwritingcheatsheet.writerrs.com

For more free tips on writing, publishing and content marketing, visit my blog at writerrs.com/blog

The Author Effect

"If the book is true, it will find an audience that is meant to read it."

—Wally Lamb

Chapter 1: Opportunity Awaits

My dream was always to become a published author. For most of my life, I thought it was a pipe dream. At that time, would-be authors needed to submit book queries to traditional publishers. You would write an outline and a few chapters. Then you would need an agent to submit your query to editors. The agent needed to convince marketing departments, who then convinced a publisher. The publisher would then need to convince bookstores to buy the book. If that went well, and they deemed your book worthy, the time between putting words on a paper and seeing the book published could take one to two years.

Pretty discouraging, but all that changed in late 2007 when Amazon's e-book publishing arm launched. Kindle Direct Publishing along with its Kindle Reader was the tipping point for the world of self-publishing. Gone were the days of dismissing self-published authors. The perception that they lacked the talent to land a book deal would gradually fade.

The Author Effect

In 2010, I discovered that my dream of being a published author could become a reality. Kindle Readers were becoming more and more popular. Indie authors were prospering like never before, and I learned it was entirely possible to become a profitable published author. I no longer needed to wait for a publisher to choose me. The gates were open. I just needed to learn how to open them. When Amazon set a place at the table for authors, they disrupted the publishing industry forever. This gave more would-be authors the freedom to flourish outside of the traditional publishing model. Until recently, most people believed that self-publishing on Amazon was for wannabes who weren't really good at writing and couldn't get signed by a publisher. Today, many self-published authors choose to be self-published and turn down traditional publishing houses by choice.

The truth is, most people want to get signed by a publisher because they feel it validates them as an author. It has very little to do with the benefits that publishers actually provide. It reassures them that their work has value. A big publisher deems them worthy, and that feels great. It's natural. Everyone wants recognition. It builds our confidence to know how meaningful, helpful and brilliant our book is. But did you know that the publisher takes most of the book royalties? That they do almost zero marketing of your book? You have very little creative liberty? You lose the rights to your book? If you don't sell enough books, you're often required to payback your advance or buy back unsold copies of your book? To make matters worse, it's nearly impossible to get signed with a publisher as a new writer. Without the reach of an established author, a new writer is a risky investment in a publisher's eyes. Even if it's the best book ever written. Now more than ever, it makes so much more sense to self-publish than to try to land a book deal with a traditional publisher.

My very first book was an experiment. I knew I wanted to write non-fiction books, so I decided to start with a cookbook. I had no idea what I was doing, but I used it as a way to teach myself how to use the Kindle Direct Publishing platform to publish and market a book. I learned so much in the process, and looking back on it now, I made it much more time-consuming than necessary. For example, I took my own photos for every single recipe because I thought that would make the book better, but I later learned it was totally unnecessary. The file size with photos made it more expensive to produce, which cut into my profits. Not only that, the images were not good enough to include in the print version. I learned so many valuable lessons from that first book, and all the mistakes were well worth it when I wrote my other books. That first little cookbook was my education and the birth of my little publishing empire. Each book I release increases my income because it works with Amazon's algorithm to cause more readers to find me. What's more, my books lead me to new opportunities that would not be possible otherwise. The idea for my first bestselling book, *Airbnb Toolbox*, came to me because I had a successful side hustle as an Airbnb Host and thought it would be a good topic to educate other people on how to do it too. That little book showed me the power of what a published book can do for you. I received exposure that I never would have had if I hadn't written a book about it. Specialty publications contacted me for interviews, I was able to secure affiliate marketing relationships with vendors, and my Airbnb bookings increased. On top of that, my book royalties offset many of the costs associated with running my Airbnb business. That's when I realized I needed to publish books for my main copywriting business.

My other books, *Online Learning & Course Design* and *Mighty Writers,* are bestsellers in their respective categories, and they helped me take my business to the next level. I gained speaking opportunities, and I was able command a higher fee for my services. In this book I want to help you do the same. I want you to enjoy the same kind of rewards that I've enjoyed. I want you to be able to leverage your book to accomplish any future goals you decide on - which, in turn, will transform your book into something much more than words on a page. The goal of this book is to help you realize these same things: opportunity, confidence and sense of accomplishment that publishing a book can bring you. This book is the map that will help you level up your business with a published book. I always keep the information in this book updated on the latest changes with Amazon publishing, so it's filled with tried and true, time-tested tips from my own personal experience . . . not theory and outdated information. I've been publishing on Amazon since 2010, and I'm still publishing on Amazon today. I don't make empty promises. I just share what I've learned and what's worked for me, so that you can give yourself the best chance for success.

"Every secret of a writer's soul, every experience of his life, every quality of his mind, is written large in his works."

—Virginia Woolf

Chapter 2: What Is Your Why?

Before you decide on your book topic, you need to figure out your why. What is the purpose of your book? What is your end goal and why is it important to you? Be specific. When you become a published author, it leads to greater success in your business. People are impressed when you're an author. It opens doors for you. You get inquiries from people wanting to work with you instead of having to chase clients. They get to know you through your book and want to work with you. That's why it's important to decide what you want your book to accomplish for your business. You'll have a more cohesive brand message and more clarity in exactly what problems you solve for your clients. The process of writing a book will force you to think about:

- What you do with your clients from start to finish.
- Who your target audience is.
- What makes you different.

To differentiate your brand, your book needs to help your readers think differently about a problem. It should make them more aware and turn on some light bulbs in their minds. When you offer a fundamental distinction, it will make you more memorable. People will know, like and trust you. When you have a book, you can hand it to potential clients. You won't need to explain your business. You can simply hand them your book to learn more about what you do.

When it comes to royalties, it's important to have the right expectations. While we would love it, and it's not impossible, your book will probably not make you rich. If you choose a topic that people want to learn about, you can still earn royalties, plus there are so many other benefits to writing a book. It will be a powerful marketing asset for your business, giving you a platform for new opportunities.

So rather than focus on book sales, what business outcomes do you want your book to create? Do you want to gain exposure for your business? Improve your credibility in your marketplace? Do you want speaking opportunities? Are you looking to fulfill a personal passion project? To attract more clients? To attract higher-end clients? To sell a product? Lead people to make an appointment? Fill a workshop? If you don't know where you're headed, how do you expect to get there? After you know your why, it's easier to decide what you want to write about. Whatever the purpose, it has to be a strong enough motivator to supply you with the discipline and drive you'll rely on when writing your book. Your purpose must be much larger than words on a page for it to serve you well.

Here are some of the why's for publishing a non-fiction book:

Why #1: Business Growth - Writing a book can be a great revenue generator and an effective way to capture leads if you are building a business. That said, it's important to have a long term perspective if this is your goal. Don't make money the only reason you're writing a book. If your only goal is to make a certain amount of money by a certain date, you'll pile on the stress. To make matters worse, you'll strain the writing process. That's not the best foundation to build on. Instead, look at earning royalties and getting leads from your book as a long-term investment. Your readers have already bought your book. Now you have the opportunity to get them to buy from you again.

Why #2: Improve Credibility - If you want to gain credibility in your field, a book is the perfect starting point. It provides proof on the value of your knowledge and insights. Even better, your book can serve as a powerful business card. When you're meeting your dream clients, you can give them a copy of your book instead of a card that they'll easily toss away or lose in the mix of the others. It's mere existence will work for you all the time. When people see it on their desk, they'll think of you. It's an ongoing a reminder that will prompt them to contact you before anyone else.

Why #3: Expand Your Reach - Your book can help you connect with influential people in your industry, such as other authors, podcasters and journalists who can expand your network in new ways. When you have a best-selling book, it gives you the perfect reason to talk to key people in your industry and have others reach out to you. Becoming an author opens up connections to new and interesting people and increases your exposure.

Why #4: Share Your Passion - You might simply want to share your knowledge, experience, or research about a certain topic because you want to enlighten others. Perhaps you're looking to create awareness or raise money for a charity. You might have a personal experience that directly relates to a cause. You can use your passion as the foundation for your first book. If this is you, remember to be specific about why you're so passionate about it.

Why #5: Tell A Story - You might have a story to tell. Whether it's a guide to solving a problem, or a story of someone else who solved a problem. No matter what the story, you can use it to make a difference in the lives of others. Why not share it? You never know what impact it may have.

Regardless of your why for writing a book, a clear vision will make your writing much clearer and prevent you from losing focus. So, take the time to find your why.

"The amateur believes he must first overcome his fear; then he can do his work. The professional knows that fear can never be overcome."

— The War of Art

Chapter 3: Let Nothing Stand In Your Way

Hopefully I've convinced you how great self-publishing is, but there's another obstacle to overcome before you get started: your attitude. As a new writer, you'll need to identify any doubts and fears that might get in your way. All writers deal with doubt and fear when they first decide to write a book. It's so easy to let these thoughts take over and prevent you from writing the book. Here are some common fears:

Fear #1 - I'm Not Enough Of An Expert

The good news is you don't need a fancy degree or prestigious award to share your personal experience. The most effective books share stories of transformation or personal experience: Why you do what you do. How you've used your knowledge and skills to help others. The process you worked through to improve and grow. The more personal the experience, the more people will connect with your message. Your personal experience is much powerful than you realize. You don't need to be anointed an "expert" in order to help people with what you have to say. As long as you provide value, your readers will appreciate your book.

Fear #2 - I'm Not A Good Writer

This is one of the most common fears people have when thinking about writing a book. I get it. If you never liked writing in school, or never felt you had a knack for it, it's hard to think about writing a book. But if you can tell a story, you can write a book. Think of it as telling stories instead of writing. You're sharing your experience with others so they can benefit from it. A book is simply a collection of stories. The most important thing to think about when writing your book is getting the first draft *done*, not perfect. You can always go back and improve anything you write later because it's never set in stone. You can fix any mistakes as soon as they arise. This is a big benefit in today's era of self-publishing. You can upload an updated version of your book anytime you want. So don't sweat the small stuff. Don't stop writing to look for that "perfect word." The main goal is to finish your first draft. So keep writing!

Fear #3 - I Don't Have Time

Books don't need to take a long time to write, so it's okay if you're busy. I wrote my first book in a month and my second in three weeks. One was 110 pages and the other 75 pages. The number one reason most people don't finish writing a book is because they make it a much bigger project than it really needs to be. Remember, you don't need to share everything you know in one book. You're not trying to solve all the problems - just one. If you have a really big idea, take one small section of that big idea and distill what you know down to one simple message.

A shorter, more focused book will be easier to write and more engaging for the reader. You'll set yourself up for success in actually finishing your book, and you won't overwhelm your reader with too much information. There is so much competition today for people's attention, which is why shorter books are actually more successful.

Many books sold on Amazon today are shorter than 50,000 words. A manuscript of 18,000 - 20,000 words is still long enough to print in paperback. So for a 20,000 word book you would need to write 667 words per day to complete it in 30 days - that's very doable!

I've simplified the writing process, so you can easily write your first book in thirty days, with approximately one hour per day blocked out for writing. Don't think you have that much time? Look for ways you can get some time back. How much time do you spend on social media or watching TV? These time-consuming activities will always be there, but now is the time to pursue being an author.

Fear #4 - I Don't Have The Technical Skills

You don't need to be a tech genius or expert in social media savant to publish your first book successfully. The process takes some learning and understanding, but it's very doable. As long as you have some level of familiarity with basic technology and social media, you can do this. My step-by-step tips in this book will help you with the details.

Fear #5 - Now Is Not The Right Time

Many would be authors who want to write a book will say "the timing isn't right." They plan on writing a book "someday," or "next year," when "the timing is right," as if the passing of time will magically change things. Time passes, and they're just as busy, or busier than before. The truth is, there's never the perfect time. The stars will never align. You'll never have unlimited free time to write your book. You simply have to start, no matter what. You can never prepare enough, and you'll never be totally "ready" to work on your book.

Fear #6 - What If My Book Fails? I'll Look Foolish.

This is a fear that people have the hardest time getting over, especially when writing a book for their business. What if you invest all your time on a book, and it's not worth it? What if nobody cares about it or wants to read it? We'll talk about the importance of validating your book idea in the next chapter, so you can set it up for success.

"It's not the writing part that's hard. What's hard is sitting down to write.

What keeps us from sitting down is Resistance."

— The War of Art

Chapter 4: Selecting a Profitable Topic

Did you know you probably have four to five books inside you right now? You have the knowledge in your head already through your experiences. It's just hidden within your daily routine. You can write about anything. The possibilities are endless, but you'll need to think strategically and not rush this part of the process. You want to make sure that it's a topic people are searching for and isn't too competitive.

When writing non-fiction, the common advice when getting started is to write about something you know a lot about. When I wrote *Airbnb Toolbox*, the topic came easily for me because I already knew so much about it. I had developed my own processes that helped me run my Airbnb side business effectively and efficiently, so it was easy to share what I had learned with others. I knew the topic so well, that it was easy for me to write a book on it. In the book I share what works well for me, including tools such as my email templates, checklists and cheatsheets. The idea was to make it as easy as possible for a new host to get started easily and avoid the pitfalls when first getting started. I invested the necessary time to make it a high quality book so that it received positive reviews. It's one of my most successful books and continues to sell consistently everyday.

The best way to get started on finding your book idea is to brainstorm. Set aside fifteen minutes to write out book ideas. Keep writing. Don't erase anything. Allow your ideas to flow freely. If nothing's coming to you, just keep writing. Anything. Don't criticize and judge. Just write and keep your pen moving. Write for a full fifteen minutes even if it means writing that you are tired and want to stop writing. Think about your passions, interests, areas of expertise and anything else that pops into your mind at that moment.

Set a timer for fifteen minutes and begin to free-write about each area. If you can write on that one topic non-stop for fifteen minutes, you probably know enough to write a book about it.

While some people struggle to transform this activity into an actual book topic, others have an endless amount of ideas swimming around. While this might be a good problem, it can be difficult to decide which book to write first. If you're struggling with picking your first topic, ask yourself these questions:

- Which topic do you know the most about, making it easier and quicker to write?
- Which topic makes you the most excited?

If after the brainstorm you still don't come up with a book idea that's right for you, don't worry. Take a break for a day and go through the free-writing exercise again. You might need to revisit it several times before finding a topic idea that truly resonates with you. After you've narrowed down a topic, you'll want to research it so you can find out if it will rank on Amazon and resonate with readers. You can do this by using some keyword research tools.

Here are the free and paid tools that I use:

- Keyword Finder
- Google Keyword Planner
- Keyword Explorer
- SEM Rush
- Publisher Rocket, formerly called KDP Rocket

Simply type in your topic ideas and the tools will give you a list of keywords and show you how many people are searching for those terms. After determining if people are searching for that topic, you'll want to find out if they're willing to pay for it. I use Publisher Rocket (KDP Rocket) to make this process easy. This is a paid tool, but I feel it's well worth the cost. You can use it to research the bestselling books in any category so you'll know exactly how many books on a topic are selling. This will help you have an accurate idea of the selling potential of your book idea. It just makes sense to make sure there is a market for your book before you write it.

Chapter 5: How To Write Your Book In A Month

The idea of sitting down and writing an entire book can be daunting, especially when you have a business to run, family obligations and other responsibilities. I'm here to tell you that you can write a book in one month. You just need a plan. Here are the steps:

Step 1: Write an outline

This will become your Table of Contents. It will be your plan so you don't go off in other directions. You will eventually expand on that structure to create your manuscript. This will become your writing roadmap.

When you sit down to write each day, you'll know exactly what to write. The more detailed you make this plan, the more quickly and easily you'll write your book. You won't spend time staring at your computer screen wondering what to write or what comes next. You'll know because it will be right there in your writing plan. You'll just follow the map to your destination.

It's also helpful to take a look at the Table of Contents of some other books on your topic. Determine which of these chapters you will cover, and which ones do not fit in your book. For more ideas, think of the topic from your reader's point of view. If you knew nothing about this topic, what would you want to see in the book?

Step 2: Research

You might think you can write your book off the top of your head because you're the expert on the topic, but you'll still need to do some research. When writing a non-fiction book, you want to provide the best possible resource for your readers. Your ideas and experiences are just one part of the topic, so you'll want to to expand on some areas within your subject. That will require research. You also may need to search for details such as a company name, a fact, or a quote, a book title, etc. These tasks could slow down your process.

How to Conduct Research Efficiently

Preparing ahead of time can keep you on track rather than getting sidetracked perusing the internet. If you do all your research up front, it avoids spending all your writing time going down rabbit holes. That's why starting with a detailed outline is important.

For each item in your outline, brainstorm the possible research you need and keep a list of everything you need to do. When you start the actual writing of your book, if you find you need more research, don't stop writing. Instead, create brackets in your manuscript that say [research here] and highlight them in yellow. Later, do a search within your document for the term "research" and fill in the gaps. You may want to set aside a certain amount of time per week for this. You don't want to come to the end of 30 days with a manuscript filled with research gaps.

Another option, is to do your research after you've written a section. Use the same process — create brackets that say [research here] and highlight the areas where research is needed. You can then go back and do the research in those spots after you've finished writing that section. Use the "find" function and look for the word "research" to find the areas where you need to research. The advantage to breaking up your research as you write is that you may find additional material to add to your book as your researching another topic. If you choose to research as you write you need to be careful of getting distracted and spending all your writing time doing research.

Choose Your Sources

When writing a non-fiction book, you want to make sure your sources are accurate and truthful. Just because something shows up on Google doesn't mean it's credible. Here are some ways you can properly research your topic:

- **Interviews** - Ask questions of an expert on areas you feel need expanding upon. You can do this by phone, Skype, or email. This is a great opportunity to use quotes to add to your book's credibility. Write a list of informed questions ahead of time. The idea is to augment your own research — not use the interview as the basis for all of your research. To find experts to interview, you can find bloggers on the topic using a Google search. You can also sign up as a writer on the website helpareporter.com. You can send out requests on the information you're looking for, and people who would like to be interviewed will contact you to let you know why they are interested and how they can help you. Make sure to include the person's name, title and website when referencing your interviewee.

- **Other Books** - Visit your local library to find specialized books on your topic. Many public libraries and university libraries have extensive reference books covering a wide range of topics. You can also reference other authors who have written books on your topic. It's helpful to read many books on a topic you want to write about so you can gain insight from other people's work. Read the reviews of those books to learn what readers may have liked and disliked about them.

- **Newspaper Articles** - If you're looking for facts to support your material, consult reliable newspapers. Make sure you're using well-respected publications before you cite them in your book. You can search online for news articles on the subject you're covering.

- **Industry Websites** - For authoritative information, refer to credible sites industry or government sites. Use narrow keywords to locate the specific information you are searching for.

When conducting research it's important to stay organized. Keep all of your research in one location — whether it's in a folder on your computer, or using a digital organizational tool such as Evernote or Asana.

Step 3: Set A Realistic Time Frame

The next step is to schedule your writing time with yourself. If you're a business owner or entrepreneur, you don't have a year to devote to writing a book. You might not be able to spend hours a day working on your book. You need to get it done quickly in a way that fits your schedule.

Start by setting a realistic amount of time each day to work on your book. I suggest setting aside 45 minutes to 90 minutes a day to work on your book. When you know what you're going to write using these steps, this should be plenty of time. One of the biggest reasons people take a long time writing a book is they don't know what they want to write, or they try to cover too much information.

Also keep in mind that a research based book takes longer to write because you have to study, evaluate and determine your opinion of the studies. Writing from your own experiences takes less time. While you may draw on anecdotes, or refer to an occasional quote or information from a book, the material comes from your head. You will only need to write about a process you created, or your area of expertise.

When planning your writing time, you'll need to learn how long it takes you to write. You might normally write 750 words per hour, but the topic you've chosen could slow you down to 500 words per hour. Or you might speed up to 1,000 words per hour. Think about how long it might take to compose your daily word count goal. For example, if you're writing a book that's 100 pages long, that's about 30,000 words. If your goal is to write your book in 30 days, you'll need to write 1,000 words a day. Make sure you factor in time for research, interviews and editing. You'll also want to allow some extra time for unforeseen circumstances. Another option is to plan your writing based on chapters. For instance, you could set a goal for writing a chapter a day, if you have the time available.

Step 4: Set A Writing Schedule

Now that you've laid the foundation with a writing plan for your book, it's time to sit down and start writing. You already have your outline as your Table of Contents, so you have a path to follow. You'll need to make an appointment with yourself and stick to it - even if it's at night when everyone else is sleeping!

Writing consistently helps you keep a rhythm going. If you put it aside for long periods of time, you'll get out of the flow. You'll have to refresh your memory every time you back to it. Make that time sacred. When you write consistently you'll be surprised at how fast the process goes.

Nothing other than an emergency should take you away from writing your book during those scheduled writing blocks.

Here are some tips to help you:

- Find a quiet place to write.
- Limit distractions.
- Keep your appointments with yourself.
- Always back up your work!! Use Google Drive or Dropbox in case of computer crashes, power outages, etc. You never know what could happen.

Make A Commitment To Yourself

It's important to have an attitude that supports meeting your goal. You must:

- Be willing to do what it takes.
- Stay optimistic.
- Remain objective.
- Be tenacious - don't let anything get in the way of finishing your book.
- Don't sacrifice quality by rushing it, but stick to your writing schedule.
- If you stay committed, you will finish your book.

Expand Each Point on Your Outline

Start the process by expanding on each of the points on your outline. Add your own stories, personal experiences or insights to help make the topic come alive. This is where you bring your unique perspective to the topic. This keeps your book interesting and engaging instead of dull and boring. A simple trick is to finish each point you make with a story. You can work on the chapters in any order that you choose.

To make the process go faster, try speaking your book using the voice recognition in Google Docs. When expanding on a point or telling a story, just speak as if you're talking to a friend. This will save you TONS of time. You can also speak into your smartphone using the voice recognition. If you have an iPhone, you can record it into an email to yourself and copy and paste it into your document later. I often do this when a thought comes to mind when I'm in the car or away from my computer. You can also speak your book into a digital recorder and have it professionally transcribed. By dictating your book, you'll write substantially more words for your first draft.

Because we don't always speak the same way we would write something, you'll need to go back and edit the transcription on your document so that it reads well as a book.

I recommend that you avoid the temptation to edit as you write. If you interrupt your flow by evaluating each and every word choice and sentence structure, you'll lose momentum. Instead, just keep writing words on the page. Don't stop to edit anything. This practice will help you become a more creative and productive writer. Remember it's okay to write a "bad" first draft. You'll refine and edit it later. This is just the first draft.

"Whatever you can do, or
dream you can, begin it.
Boldness has genius, magic,
and power in it. Begin it now."

— W.H. Murray

Chapter 6: Edit And Revise

Once you've finished expanding on each point of your outline for your first draft, you can then begin to edit and revise your work. A simple trick to edit your writing is to read it out loud. It's one of the best ways to catch errors. You also want to have at least three other people review your proofread your work.

Step 1: Start With Words On Paper

For your first draft you're focusing on getting words on paper as quickly as possible. Remember, don't stop to edit, just keep writing. The point is to keep moving forward and get the words out. If you start editing too soon, you'll stall the process.

Step 2: Quick Editing

You can begin quick edits of your work after you complete your first draft. Another option is to do quick edits at the end of each daily writing session. Either way, the point is to keep the momentum going and not interrupt your writing by editing too soon. For quick editing, look for the following:

- Make sure all the content is included. Have you left anything out?
- Does it flow well? Is it in logical order? Does the structure make sense?
- Are there any inconsistencies or major mistakes?

Step 3: In-Depth Editing

After your quick editing, you can start in-depth editing. Read every chapter again and ask yourself these questions:

• What point am I trying to make? Is this point necessary?

• Is it coming across clearly? Is it as simple as it can be?

• Is it as short as it can be? Did I forget to include necessary information?

Look at your book from the reader's point of view. Make any changes that will improve the experience for your reader. Do that for every chapter. Then do it for every paragraph. This will make sure your writing is sharp and concise.

Step 4: Read Aloud

Once you've gone through your entire book, print your manuscript read the entire book again — but this time read it aloud. This will help you catch any mistakes, grammatical errors and issues you missed the first time. Hearing yourself speak the words will highlight bad word choices and odd phrasing. As you read it aloud, make notes in the margins where you need to make changes.

It's also helpful to have two or three other people read your manuscript and provide you with honest feedback. Another set of eyes will catch things you will not notice. Ask them to read your book as if they did not know you. If you get the same feedback from more than one person, you'll want to take it seriously and rework it.

Go back and make any necessary edits and give it a final proofread for typos and errors. Once you've gone through all the above steps, you should have a manuscript that's ready to format and publish.

"You don't write because you want to say something.

You write because you have something to say."

—F. Scott Fitzgerald

Chapter 7: Setting Up Your KDP Listing

We'll now turn our attention to how to set up your book listing on KDP in the best way possible so you can maximize sales. From your KDP Dashboard, under the area that says "Create New Title," select "Kindle ebook." Amazon will then lead you through the process to set up your ebook. By following the prompts, you'll complete each section and upload your book file and cover file to publish your book on Amazon. On the first screen, it will ask you to enter your book details, on the second screen you'll upload your manuscript file and cover. On the third screen, you'll enter your pricing information. After you complete each step for your ebook, you'll repeat the steps for your paperback version. You'll go back to your KDP Dashboard and select "Paperback." Most of the steps will be automatically populated with the information you entered for your ebook.

Let's take a look at each screen and how to complete each area properly:

Screen 1: Book Details

The first section contains fields to enter the following details of your book:

Language:

Here you'll select the primary language of your book. This is the language you wrote your book in.

Your Book Title

There's an art and science to naming your book on your Amazon listing. Your title and subtitle need to clearly state what it's about. When properly worded, it also helps you carve out a spot in the marketplace. This is where topic research and keyword research becomes important. Simple choices and tweaks can result in hundreds of additional visitors, which equates to more sales. Also, make sure what you enter in this field matches what is on your cover design.

Here are some important tips for an optimized title:

- It needs to be clear, more than catchy. You may need to revise the working title that you wrote earlier to optimize it properly.
- The title and subtitle should work together to sell the solution to your customers' problem, or show a way to make their lives better.
- It must incorporate **keywords** that will attract your ideal customer. If people can't find your book, they won't buy it. The proper use of keywords helps shoppers find your book.

When people shop for a book on Amazon, they generally go to the search bar at the top of Amazon and describe the type of book they are looking for. Amazon uses these keywords that the customer typed to decide which books should be shown to the customer. Understanding keywords, and being smart with them, should always be a part of your self-publishing plan. Discovering what keywords people type into Amazon's search bar will give you a good idea if people are actively searching for your book topic.

You can use Amazon auto selection to help identify search terms for your topic on Amazon. Auto selection populates the search bar with words Amazon believes you will type in next, based on previous customers' searches and your own.

First, you want to start by going into incognito mode. This will make sure that the information Amazon presents you is not based on your search history. Amazon likes to track what we do, click and buy. And they use this information in order to show us things. When doing keyword research, you don't want that to happen. You want to know what everyone else is doing and see their raw results.

Next, select "Kindle Store" or "Books" as the Amazon category. You want to know what is popular in your industry and not be shown product terms instead of book terms.

Once you have "Kindle Store" or "Books" selected, start typing in words or phrases that pertain to your book. Type slowly. You want to give Amazon an opportunity to pre-generate a list of potential keywords for you. You can do this with every letter of the alphabet – even 'z' – and look to see how Amazon completes your search phrase. You'd be surprised what Amazon will come up with. As you go, keep a written list of possible keywords that you think would pertain to your book. Your goal is to find words that are frequently searched but not overly competitive. A good strategy is to add each letter of the alphabet at the end of your word/phrase and see what comes up. That should give you a pretty good list of words, but let's go one step further and look at Google's information as well. This will helps you learn more about the volume of searches on that topic. If you find a lot of people are searching for that same subject on Google, it's more likely to be a good idea for a book topic.

Start by going to KWFinder.com. It gives more information about the popularity of the term and general competition. You can do a couple of searches there for free each day.

Type in a word/phrase into the keyword tool and see what it presents. Go through the list and write down any that you think might be good for your book. Once you have a list of Google words, go back to Amazon and type those words in to see what Amazon suggests. If nothing is shown, it means that even though it might be searched on Google, it doesn't translate over to Amazon. You can also do the same thing with the other tools I mentioned, using their free versions:

- Google Keyword Planner
- Keyword Explorer
- Keyword Finder
- SEMRush.com

Again, my favorite tool is Publisher Rocket. For a one time fee, you can perform even more extensive research on Kindle keywords and category selection. It gives you specific insights into keyword competitiveness and how many people are searching for it on Amazon.

Series

In this area you will indicate if your book is part of a series. There are some marketing advantages for writing a series of books on a topic. The first is you can ask Amazon to create a product bundle of all of your books in the series, which can generate more sales. The second is you can add a call to action inside your book for your readers to purchase the next book in the series. Amazon has some requirements for creating a book series bundle, so it's important to have this in mind ahead of time if you think you might want to do this. I know this from first hand experience because I made this mistake. Although I knew I wanted to write a series of books, I didn't know about Amazon's requirements, so I didn't plan them out properly. Even though I filled in the "Series" area, I didn't have the proper elements in place for Amazon to approve the series as a bundle. For a book series to be created successfully, Amazon looks for the following:

- Titles grouped together that follow a sequential pattern, with volume numbers in an ordered series.
- All book descriptions, cover images and book features must have a visible continuation among the titles, so that customers can make an informed decision.
- Inside content of the book must clearly relate to the other books and mention the other books in the series.

So make sure to include these elements if you're planning on writing several books on your topic.

Edition Number

An edition is a particular version of a book. The edition number tells readers whether the book is an original version or an updated version. If this is the first time you have published this book, enter the number 1. If the book was previously published and the version you are publishing contains significant changes, enter the number 2 (and so on).

Author

Enter your name exactly how you want it to appear on your Amazon Author Page.

Contributors

Add any other authors who may have contributed to the writing of your book, if applicable.

Description

A properly written book description is key to optimizing your listing. It's the sales page for your book. If you get this wrong, it could mean the difference between selling many copies of your book everyday, or watching it go unnoticed in a sea of other books on Amazon. Customers view your book description as they shop on Amazon. Often, it is a reader's first experience with the content of your book. A well-written description helps readers find your book. Then, it captures their interest and assures them that your book is of high quality. After that, it compels them to take the next step of hitting the buy button. Most people read the book description to decide if the book is something they want to read — then, it can go one of two ways:

Result 1: A shopper is drawn in by the first sentence of the description. After reading through the first paragraph, he or she has decided to buy the book — and keeps reading the description because it's so interesting. The shopper glances at the number of stars and is reassured because there aren't many 1 and 2 star reviews.

Result 2: The book cover caught the shopper's attention, and enticed him or her to read the description. Unfortunately, the shopper couldn't tell what the book was about and quickly became bored reading the description. The shopper moved on, leaving your page to find something else.

The results you get depend on how you write the description. Many authors simply don't spend enough time writing their book description. They think they need to summarize the entire book, and they get stalled. Remember this when writing your description: You don't need to **summarize** your book. You need to **sell** your book. If you put the time into writing a winning book description, you will maximize your sales. Sometimes even small tweaks will lead to an uptick in sales.

Make sure you include the following four elements in your book description:

1. A Headline That Draws People In

Amazon displays only the first few lines of your description, so you have limited space to encourage shoppers to click on your book to find out more. If you don't grab their attention right away, you've already lost them. The key to a headline that grabs attention is to include keywords that people will immediately recognize. It needs to entice people to hit "Read More" with a motivating first line. You can do this using one of these proven techniques:

- **Ask a question** - this is a simple way to get the attention of your ideal audience. Ask them a question about something they care about. What is burning in the minds of your target audience? What do they need an answer for? You can frame it in a story format that prompts us to ask "how?" and leads us to read more so we can answer our own question.

- **Make a promise that finally solves their problem** - offer a solution so good that they're compelled to find out if it could possibly be true.

Remember, the first sentence is your first impression. Make it count. It's as simple as turning their number one problem into a question or a promise.

2. A Blurb That Tells People What It's About

You want to explain exactly what your book is about and why it's worthwhile. Answer the following three questions:

- What problem, challenge, or question does your book address?

- How does your book solve or answer this topic?

• What exactly will readers take away from your book?

Avoid over-using superlatives. This can come across as insincere and cliche. If you say that your book is the greatest resource of all time on a subject, make sure you have evidence to back up your claim.

3. A Close That Tells People Why Your Book Is Right For Them

The end of your book description should prompt browsers to buy your book. If they've made it this far, you have their interest. Now explain why they should read your book next. Motivate readers to choose your book by connecting with you as the author and developing their trust in you. Tell us who you are. Are you an expert in your field? Do you have special insight into a topic no one else does? Tell us right away. Make us a proposition. Paint a picture of what we might get out of your book. Speak directly to the reader, and appeal to emotion. Restate what readers will get out of the book and invite them to dive in. The conclusion is also a great place to include any previous reviews from readers you may know. A descriptive pull quote from a satisfied reader is an effective way to provide a word of mouth recommendation. This is especially helpful when your book is new and you don't have any reviews yet.

4. Proper Use of Keywords Throughout

Just as you incorporated keywords into your book title, you also want to naturally include keywords in your book description. They will help your book show up in the search results when shoppers type them into Amazon's search engine. Keep in mind you must do this properly so as not to turn off potential readers. Use keywords where they make sense. Don't stuff keywords needlessly or unnaturally into your description. They should flow naturally in the sentence. Keywords should never be obvious. Repeating your Amazon keywords in your blurb can help make your book rank higher for these keywords. But be careful to avoid keyword-stuffing, as it is heavily penalized. As long as your title and product description are relevant and natural to read, it shouldn't cause a problem.

Publishing Rights

In this section you will choose between two options:

- **I own the copyright and I hold the necessary publishing rights.** Choose this option if your book is under copyright and you hold the necessary rights for the content being published.
- **This is a public domain work.** Select this option if you are publishing a public domain book. Keep in mind that the duration of copyright varies between countries/ regions. So, if your book is in the public domain in one country/region but not another, you must identify your territory rights accordingly.

Keywords

Using the keyword research you conducted earlier, enter up to 7 search terms that describe your book. Search keywords help readers find your book when they browse the Amazon site. You can enter keywords or short phrases that describe your book and are relevant to its content. The best keywords are those that do not repeat words in the title, category, or description - as you've already used them to help readers find your book. Select some additional keywords to use in this area. All keyword must comply with Amazon's Terms & Conditions. Some types of keywords are prohibited and may result in content being removed from sale. Here are some examples:

- Information covered elsewhere in your book's metadata (title, contributors, etc.)
- Subjective claims about quality (e.g. "best novel ever")
- Time-sensitive statements ("new," "on sale," "available now")
- Information common to most items in the category ("book")
- Spelling errors
- Variants of spacing, punctuation, capitalization, and pluralization ("80GB" and "80 GB," "computer" and "computers", etc.). Exception: Words translated in more than one way (e.g. "Mao Zedong" or "Mao Tse-tung," "Hanukkah" or "Chanukah"
- Anything misrepresentative like the name of an author not associated with your book. This kind of information can create a confusing customer experience. Kindle Direct Publishing has a zero tolerance policy for

metadata that is meant to advertise, promote, or mislead.

- Quotation marks in search terms. Single words work better than phrases, and specific words work better than general ones. If you enter "complete sales sequence," only people who type all of those words will find your book. For better results, enter this: complete sales sequence. That way, customers can search for any of those words and find your book.

- Amazon program names like as "Kindle Unlimited" or "KDP Select"

Categories

Books on Amazon are grouped by topic and then in several sub-topics. In this section, you'll choose from several topics and subtopics from the drop down menu. A browse category is the section of the Amazon site where users can find your book. Think of the browse category like the sections of a physical bookstore (fiction, history, and so on). You can select up to two browse categories for your book. Precise browse categorization helps readers find your book, so be sure to select the most appropriate categories for your book. Keep in mind, Amazon regularly changes these categories, so you may see a book similar to yours in a category that's no longer offered. When determining the right category, you'll want to pick subject areas that are appropriate to your book and not too competitive. By narrowing down the category as much as possible, you can rank higher in that category. Selecting the right categories can help boost your rankings, or you can approach it all wrong. If you choose a category that's so obscure, you won't find many people browsing that category. A better approach is to look at all the available categories that are appropriate for your book and choose the one that isn't too competitive, but searched often enough. If your book ranks well in the right category, it can have a huge impact on your sales. If it ranks in the top ten of its category, it will prove worthy enough for Amazon to show it to customers in other places.

Note: You can select up to 10 categories for your book through *Contact Us* within Amazon Author Central. Make sure to select the phone call option, and they will call you within minutes. You will then tell them what categories you want your book added to. You can use KDP Rocket to research the best categories. It's important to have your list ready when they call you. Here are some tips for selecting the right category:

Instead of starting with the general options Amazon shows you, do some research ahead of time. Using one of your most relevant keywords, search the Kindle Store for competing books. Take a look at the categories of the books most similar to yours. Make a list of these categories. Next, find a category that's not competitive and a category that's very competitive. You can do this by looking at the sales rank for the book in the number one spot and the ranking for the book in the number 10 spot. For example, in one category you may need a sales ranking of 95,000 to be a bestseller — not too competitive. In another category, you may need a ranking of 20 to become a bestseller — very competitive. You'll notice that many of the categories you see do not appear in the choices when setting up your book. This is because there are restricted categories and those that have keyword requirements to be listed in that category. To research categories with keyword requirements, search the KDP Help topics for "Selecting Browse Categories." Scroll down the page and click on the link for "Categories with keyword requirements." To list your book in those subcategories on Amazon.com and Amazon.co.uk, you'll need to follow the keyword requirements. Choose a marketplace and click the categories to see the keyword requirements. After you've added the required keywords, visit Author Central and click on the "Contact Us" page to request to place your book in that category. You can make this request by email or by requesting a phone conversation. Keep in mind, anytime you initiate help through Author Central, it can take anywhere from 24 hours to 2 weeks to receive a response, so you'll need to be patient.

Again, I like using KDP Rocket for identifying possible categories. It gives you real-time data showing you exactly what Amazon terms buyers search for, as well as how many other books are competing for that keyword. It helps you discover the best niche categories to help you sell more books.

If you determine the category is too competitive, or does not receive enough traffic, you can always change categories after you publish your book. A book can also be selling well, and it's beneficial to change categories to generate even more sales. If your chosen categories don't seem to be getting the results you're looking for, you can always change them.

Age and Grade Range

If you've written a children's book, you'll select the appropriate age and grade range of your ideal audience.

Pre-Order

Prior to publishing, you can offer a pre-release of your book. You'll set up the details of your pre-release on a later screen after you upload your manuscript, but I want to highlight some benefits of a pre-release — especially if you're writing a book series. Once your book is released for pre-order, there will be a live link to your book with a product page. You'll select the date you plan to release the book, and it will appear on the product page. This will allow you to continue the momentum with your readers for your book series because they can purchase it and receive it the moment it goes live. It also allows you to promote it on a blog or other channel ahead of time. Pre-orders are easier if you already have a following or audience you can offer it to. If you don't have an existing audience, you can use a pre-order to promote your book to friends and family. Keep in mind, Amazon does not allow reviews from pre-orders, but you can always include them in the "Editorial Reviews" section of your product page.

Amazon allows you to choose a release date anywhere from two weeks to 90 days out. Remember that when choosing a release date, you're committing to that date - so give yourself plenty of time! If you miss the release date, Amazon will revoke your rights to pre-release for one year. It's also important to know that Amazon will require you to submit the completed manuscript two weeks prior to your release date — so plan accordingly! When setting up your pre-release, you'll first need to upload a draft manuscript. This proves to Amazon that you're scheduling a book that you will actually finish. Just remember to meet your deadline and upload your final manuscript by the two week deadline.

Screen 2: Book Content

The most important area of the second screen is the area where you'll upload your book manuscript file and your book cover. It will give you the option to use Kindle Create to format your files for both ebook and paperback formats. We'll review formatting your manuscript and creating a book cover in Chapters 9 and 10.

For your ebook, you'll need to elect your Digital Rights Management (DRM). This is intended to inhibit unauthorized distribution of the Kindle file of your book. Some authors want to encourage readers to share their work, and choose not to have DRM applied to their book. If you choose DRM, customers will still be able to lend the book to another user for a short period, and can also purchase the book as a gift for another user from the Kindle store. Important: Once you publish your book, you cannot change its DRM setting.

An ISBN is required for all paperback books. When publishing your paperback book, you'll need to select the option to have Amazon assign you a free KDP ISBN, or purchase your own outside of Amazon. I prefer to take advantage of the free option offered by Amazon. Next, you'll select the book size, color of paper and either matte or gloss finish. Then you'll be asked to upload your file. Amazon will review your file and highlight any issues with your manuscript.

Publisher

You can choose to leave this field blank, or add a publishing company name if you have one.

Screen 3: Book Pricing

On the final screen, you'll decide if you want to enroll in KDP Select, choose your royalty option, distribution rights and set the price of your book. Once this page is complete, you'll be ready to publish.

KDP Select Enrollment

When you're setting up your book on Amazon, you'll need to decide if you want to enroll your book in KDP Select. When you enroll your eBook in KDP Select, you're committing to making the digital format available exclusively through the Kindle Store while it's enrolled in the program. You can distribute your print book through other channels.

If you make digital version of your book available elsewhere (such as on your website or blog, or on another marketplace), it is not eligible for KDP Select.

When you're enrolled in KDP Select, you can take advantage of their promotional tools - the Free Book Promotions (readers can get your book for free during a limited time) and Countdown Deals (a limited time discount). Your book also is available through Kindle Unlimited and Kindle Owners' Lending Library - which helps you reach even more readers. These programs earn you additional revenue based on the number of pages customers read through these programs.

Kindle Unlimited (KU)

Kindle Unlimited is a program where members pay a flat monthly fee to borrow up to ten titles at a time. There is no due date, but readers must return a book before they can borrow another title. Authors who publish on KDP and have titles participating in KDP Select are eligible to receive a share of royalties from Amazon's KDP Select Global Fund. The Global Fund is an amount of money that Amazon sets aside to pay out royalties to KDP authors enrolled in KDP Select. The total fund amount changes monthly, and payouts are dependent on a variety of factors outside your control. The royalties you receive depend on the amount in the Global Fund, exchange rates, and how many pages the Kindle Unlimited subscribers read. Since e-books don't have pages to count, Amazon devised the KENP (Kindle Edition Normalized Pages) metric to figure out how much a KU subscriber has read of your e-book. You only receive royalties based on how many pages the subscriber reads the first time. So if he reads only 10 KENP pages when he first opens the book, you only get royalties on those 10 pages, not the maybe hundreds of other pages in your book that he will read sometime in the future. If you choose to not enroll your ebook in KDP Select, then you would not be eligible for KU royalties. You'll still get your regular royalties from sales of your e-book title, but you won't get any if they read your book through the KU program. This is the incentive to participate in KDP Select which, as I said earlier, requires your e-book to be exclusive to the Kindle Store. With today's consumers becoming more accustomed to subscription programs for everything, it's worth considering. Keep in mind the "borrows" in Kindle Unlimited improve your ranking. Every time someone borrows it, your ranking improves.

Kindle Online Lending Library (KOLL)

The Kindle Online Lending Library (KOLL) program allows Amazon Prime members who are Kindle owners to read one Kindle eBook title for free each month. They can take as long as they want to read that one e-book but can only have access to one title per month.

As with Kindle Unlimited, only e-books enrolled in the KDP Select are eligible for Global Fund royalties for any e-books read from the KOLL. Similarly, royalties are based on the KENP pages from the first read of the e-book. Re-read pages are not included in the total.

What is Kindle Book Lending?

Kindle Book Lending is different from the Kindle Online Lending Library. All e-books published on the KDP platform are automatically enrolled in the Kindle Book Lending program. Here's how it works:

Those who purchase Kindle e-books may lend them to family and friends for a 14-day period. During that period, the original buyer does not have access to the title. Each Kindle ebook may be loaned only one time by a Kindle ebook buyer. Only purchased titles are eligible — not those dowloaded using the KU or KOLL programs. Titles shared through Kindle Book Lending do not receive any royalties. If you enroll your e-book at the 35 percent royalty level, you can opt out of this lending program. If you enroll at the 70 percent royalty level, you cannot opt-out.

Should You Enroll in KDP Select?

While KDP Select may not be worth it for some authors, I believe it's worthwhile for a business book because the promotional tools give your book more exposure on Amazon which help it get into the hands of more readers. When you offer a free promotion, it helps boost your rankings for that period of time and allows you to gain some reviews. When I first started publishing on Amazon in the early days, the free book promotion was far more powerful than it is now — but I feel it's still an effective tool for launching a business book easily and affordably. Plus, you can still offer your print version through other channels.

Many authors do not like to be dependent on Amazon in this way. It's no secret that Amazon will do what's best for Amazon, not you. Amazon continually makes changes to its programs - which the author has no control over. That's why some authors prefer to publish their ebook in all bookstores in an attempt to build audiences elsewhere, even though Amazon has the largest market share for e-books in the U.S. There is no right or wrong answer, you just need to decide on your goals and what's best for you. You'll want to decide if you're willing to grant Amazon exclusivity in exchange for their perks, or have the ability to sell your ebooks everywhere. Whatever you decide, remember you can always sell your print book everywhere. Also, you can always change your KDP Select enrollment after 90 days.

Distribution Rights

During the setup, you'll be asked to enter the territories you hold electronic publishing rights for your eBook. If you're certain you have all rights necessary to make your book available worldwide, choose All territories (worldwide rights). This will allow customers from around the world to purchase your title on Amazon.com, Amazon.co.uk, Amazon.de, Amazon.fr, Amazon.es, Amazon.it,

Amazon.co.jp, Amazon.com.br, Amazon.com.mx, Amazon.com.au, Amazon.ca, Amazon.nl, and Amazon.in. If your book is your original content, and you've never published it before, you most likely have worldwide rights. If you don't hold worldwide rights to sell and distribute your title, choose Individual territories. Then, indicate the territories in which you hold rights. This will limit sales of your publication to those territories only.

Royalty and Pricing

Amazon gives you the choice of a 35% royalty option or 70% royalty, and it will show you your profit for each option, based on the price you enter. For the 70% option, your e-book must be priced between $2.99 and $9.99. Amazon will give you an estimate of which royalty option will be most profitable for your book, based on the sales of similar books. You can find this information where it says KDP Pricing Support. After clicking the button that reads "View Service," you'll see a graphical recommendation for your royalty option. You'll need to test different price points for your ebook and paperback to see what works best for your topic. A good starting point is to price it close to your competitors and make adjustments from there. If your goal is to expand your reach and get in front of as many readers as possible, a .99 cent ebook may help draw in more readers who might be willing to take a chance on it, as opposed to a higher priced title. If you're looking to make as much money as possible, then you'll need to determine if you can sell ten times as many ebooks at .99 cents than you can at $9.99. You'll want to experiment with different price points to determine the sweet spot for your particular book. I've found that being on the higher end of the price range can surprisingly lead to more sales — depending on the category. Also, a higher price point helps show a higher perceived value when offering a free promotion. That said — this is only true if you have good book that truly offers value to your readers.

Matchbook

Kindle MatchBook gives customers who buy your print book from Amazon the option to purchase the Kindle version for $2.99 or less. When you have a print version of your title on Amazon, you can enroll the Kindle version in Kindle MatchBook and earn Kindle Direct Publishing (KDP) royalties based on the Promotional List Price (choose from $2.99, $1.99, $0.99, or free) for any Kindle MatchBook sale.

Book Lending

This feature allows readers to lend digital books they have purchased through the Kindle Store to their friends and family. Each book may be loaned once for 14 days and will not be readable by the lender during the loan period. This is only available for Kindle ebooks purchased on Amazon.com.

If you have purchased a copy of your own book, you are welcome to lend it. However, you can only lend a title once per the terms of the Kindle Book Lending program. Loans of Kindle books are not purchases and thus are not eligible to receive royalty payments.

All KDP titles are enrolled in lending by default. For titles in the 35% royalty option, you may choose to opt out of lending by deselecting the checkbox under "Book Lending" in the book pricing & promotion section of the title setup process, but you may not choose to opt out a 70% royalty optioned title or a title included in the lending program of another sales or distribution channel.

Publish!

Once you hit Publish Your Book, you'll receive an email letting you know that Amazon will review your book listing and content. It can take up to 72 hours before you receive another email letting you know it is approved and available for purchase in the Kindle Store.

Chapter 8: Formatting Your Manuscript

From the KDP Dashboard you'll upload your book content file as part of the book listing process. Before uploading your manuscript, you'll need to format it properly for both ebook and print formats.

Formatting Your E-Book

Amazon provides a tool called Kindle Create to help you format your manuscript to publish as an ebook. It works with your word processing application (Microsoft Word, Apple Pages, or Google Docs). Whatever software you use, simply export your file to the .doc(x) format. You'll then import your file directly into Kindle Create, which will convert your file into the proper format for readers to view your book on all Kindle reading devices. It automatically detects chapter titles, adds styling to them, and makes it easy to use them to create a Kindle table of contents. You can also format paragraphs with styles, change the design style with themes, and preview how your eBook will display on tablets, phones, and Kindle E-readers. So keep the fonts and format simple in your original word processing file:

- Body text - Georgia 12
- Chapter titles - Georgia 14
- At the end of each chapter insert a page break.
- Do not use special characters or headers and footers as they will not translate to the Kindle format. You can use bold or italics.

Front Matter

The front matter should be centered with a page brake after each. It includes the following:

- Title page
- Copyright page
- List of other books you've written
- Dedication (optional)
- Call to action - we'll discuss this in Chapter 11

Back Matter

After you formatted each chapter, you'll need to decide if you want to include back matter. You can include the following:

- Description of any other books you may have written with a link to the Amazon page.

- Thank you note to your readers and an opportunity to sign up for your email list.

- A note to readers asking for a review of your book, including the link.

How To Convert Your File for Kindle

Once you have your file properly set up, Amazon has now made it relatively easy to convert your file using Kindle Create. Here's how to get started converting your book:

1. Install the Kindle Create software. To download the free software, click on "Help" located on the upper right corner of the KDP Dashboard. Next, under the Help Topics on the left hand column, click on "Prepare Your Book." On the next screen, under "ebooks" click on "Kindle Create" under Free Tools. On the next screen,

you'll choose to download Kindle Create for either PC or Mac.

2. Launch Kindle Create to begin converting your book.

3. Click the New Project from File button.

4. From the Choose File dialog box, click the Novels, Essays, Poetry, Narrative Non-Fiction option.

5. Select the language of your book.

6. Click the Choose File button, select your .doc(x) file, and click Open.

7. Kindle Create will begin converting it to a Kindle eBook.

8. Keep in mind, every page break will become a new section in your book.

9. Once you see Import Successful, click Continue.

10. Next, it will start the process of creating automatic chapter titles. Click Get Started, and Kindle Create will find possible Chapter Titles in your book.

11. You'll see a list of Suggested Chapter Titles. Uncheck any items that are not chapter headings. The checked items will become part of your clickable table of contents.

12. Select File, Save Project to save your ebook. This will save your book as a .kcb file in the folder you choose.

13. When you click Publish, Kindle Create saves it as a .kpf
    file that you can submit to KDP for publishing.

Tip: Images in your Kindle book will increase its file size.
For books in the 70% royalty option, Amazon charges an
additional 15 cents per megabyte when readers buy your
book. Also, don't copy and paste images into your Word
document. Instead, save a jpeg image to your computer.
Then, insert the picture in your Kindle Create document,
using the plus sign on the upper left of the screen. Always
align your pictures in the center and use high quality
images. While it may decrease the file size, low quality
images result in a poor reader experience. Also, when you
first open your file in Kindle Create, the spacing and fonts
might look a little funky. Don't worry, you can fine tune
everything there.

Now that we've covered formatting your Kindle ebook,
let's turn our attention to your paperback version. You'll
want to have a paperback version to hand out for business
purposes, as well as provide additional royalty income.

Formatting Your Paperback

Self-publishing a paperback on Amazon is a print on demand service, so it costs you nothing to set up. That means your book will only be printed when someone buys a copy. You don't need to purchase any copies in bulk ahead of time. To help you format your paperback, Amazon has created templates in Microsoft Word into which you can insert your content. You can find these templates, as well as all specifications for setting up your document in the KDP Dashboard. Click on "Help" located on the upper right corner. Next, under the Help Topics on the left hand column, click on "Prepare Your Book." When your pages are ready for print, you'll export the finished product as a pdf and upload it to the "paperback content" section of your KDP listing.

Printing Terms and Guidelines to Understand

Before you get started on the paperback version of your book, let's review some common printing terms and guidelines:

Trim size - This is your printed book's width and height. The most common trim size for paperbacks in the U.S. is 6" x 9" (15.24 x 22.86 cm), but you can choose other sizes.

Bleed - This means elements will extend to the edge of the page. Planning for bleed will prevent a white border at the edge of the page.

Margins - Each page has three outside margins (top, bottom, and side) and one inside margin (also called the gutter). Margins makes your text isn't cut off. Set your page size, then set your margins. Your margin size will depend on the number of pages count and on if you have elements that bleed.

Image Size - For the best results, all images should be sized at 100%, flattened to one layer and inserted into your manuscript file at a minimum resolution of 300 DPI (dots per inch). A color photo will only print in color if you selected the color ink printing option for your book.

Before you upload your manuscript to KDP, you'll need to format it so it meets Amazon's quality standards. Here's how to set up your pages using Microsoft Word:

Setting Page Size

1. On the Layout tab, in the Page Setup group, click Size, and then select More Paper Sizes. This opens a dialog box.

2. Enter your book's trim size into the Width and Height fields. For bleed: Add 0.125" (3 mm) to the width and 0.25" (6 mm) to the height. For example, if your trim size is 6" x 9" (15.24 x 22.86 cm), set the page size to 6.125" x 9.25" (15.54 x 23.46 cm).

3. In the Apply to list, select Whole document and click OK. This resizes your pages and changes your page count, which you need to know for setting your margins.

Setting Margins

1. On the Layout tab, in the Page Setup group, click Margins, and then select Custom Margins. This opens a dialog box.

2. In the Multiple pages list, select Mirror margins.

3. In the Apply to list, select Whole document.

4. Identify your margin sizes based on page count using the chart at the end of this step.

5. Enter your Top, Bottom, Inside, and Outside margins based on your book's page count. Do not enter any value into the Gutter field. Click OK.

Tip: If your page count changes, go back and check the inside margin because it may also need to change.

Modifying Styles For a Custom Look

Using the styles in Word helps you to set a consistent style that contains all the instructions for font, font color, font size, as well as horizontal and vertical spacing. You can use the preset Styles in Microsoft Word or you can modify Styles to create your own design.

This saves you time because you won't have to repeat each step for each part of your book. Once you know which Style you want to use, or which choices you want to make to create your own Style, you can begin to modify and create Styles.

Modifying the Normal Style for Book Text

The Normal style is used for your book's body text. You'll pick your font and font size as well as the alignment of each paragraph, spacing between paragraphs, and the indentation of the first line of each paragraph. These are optional style choices. You can pick these attributes based on your preferences.

1. On the Home tab, right-click the Normal style and select Modify.

2. Select your Font and Font Size from the lists.

3. Click the Format list and select Paragraph. This opens a dialog box.

4. In the dialog box:

a. Under General, set the Alignment to Justified.

b. Under Special, set First line indent to 0.2".

c. Under Spacing, set Before and After to 0 and under Line Spacing select Single

Applying the Normal Style to Book Text

1. Place the cursor before the first chapter title and then hold down the SHIFT + PAGE DOWN keys until the cursor moves to the end of your document.

2. Keep everything highlighted. On the Home tab, in the Styles ribbon, click the Normal style.

Tip: Applying the Normal style to all of the content after the front matter ensures that any hidden or unintentional formatting is changed.

Modifying the Heading 1 Style

1. On the Home tab, right-click the Heading 1 style and select Modify. This opens a dialog box.

2. Select your Font, Font Size, and Color, and set the alignment to Center.

3. Click the Format list and select Paragraph. This opens a dialog box.

4. Under Special, select (none).

5. Under Spacing, set Before and After to 60pt to move the title about a third of the way down the page and separate it from the first paragraph.

6. Click OK on both open boxes to save changes.

Tip: Depending on whether the font you chose is large (example: Arial) or a small (example: Times New Roman), you should size between 9 and 12 point. Amazon recommends 9 point for a larger font and 12 point for a smaller font.

Page Numbers

Do not place page numbers near the inside margin.

Formatting Chapters

To ensure that your content begins on the correct page, you need to use section breaks. This allows you to change the formatting of a specific section without affecting the entire document. You will add a section break between the front matter and book body to distinguish these parts of the book. You will also use section breaks so that each chapter title page starts on its own page. While you are making changes to each chapter title page, you will also apply the Heading 1 style to each chapter title. Using Heading 1 tags the chapter title so that it will appear in the table of contents.

Inserting Section Breaks

1. Place the cursor at the end of the front matter.

2. On the Layout tab, click the Breaks list and then select Next Page.

3. Repeat the previous step at the end of each chapter.

Applying Heading 1 to Chapter Titles

1. Highlight the title of the first chapter. On the Home tab, in the Styles section, click Heading 1 to apply the style to the chapter title.

2. Repeat the previous step for each chapter title.

Front Matter

Front matter consists of the sections that come before the first chapter. Some are optional, but there is a standard order. Below is a list of the elements readers may expect to see in their proper order. If you're unsure which to include, refer to books with content similar to yours as a guide.

- Half title page – right-facing page (requires blank page after)
- Title page, right-facing page
- Copyright page
- Dedication – right-facing page (requires blank page after)
- Table of Contents with page numbers, right-facing page (might require blank page after, depending on number of TOC pages)
- Foreword – right-facing page (requires blank page after)

Note: Right-facing pages are odd numbered pages in printed books because the first piece of paper is on the right side, facing up from the open, printed book. The back of the cover is the left-facing page.

Adding Section Breaks and Blank Pages

Adding blank pages ensures that all printed pages are in the proper position. Use section breaks to add blank pages within the front matter as needed. Here's how:

- Insert the cursor at the top of the page that will follow the new blank page.
- On the Layout tab, click the Breaks list and then select Next Page.
- To create a placeholder page for the table of contents, add a right-facing blank page immediately before Chapter 1 and name it Table of Contents.
- Before you start applying styles, make sure that you've added section breaks in between pages of your front matter

Tip: To make the copyright symbol, hold down the CTRL + ALT+ C keys.

Page Numbers

Do not place page numbers near the inside margin. Blank pages are part of the sequence, but should not show the number.

Chapter 9: Your Book Cover

The right book cover will set your book up for success, and you don't need to hire a professional designer to do it. I design all the covers on my books, and it costs me nothing. You can design a beautiful book cover yourself, you just need to make sure it includes all the essential elements.

Set up a free account Canva and start creating! You can choose from their templates, or design your own. Once you've designed your cover, simply save your image and upload it to Amazon's free Cover Creator tool. You can also use the templates in Amazon's Cover Creator. It allows you to customize your cover with a variety of layouts and fonts. You'll access the Cover Creator when you get to the "Paperback Content" section when setting up your book on KDP.

Note: Your paperback cover will need to be created separately as it needs a spine and a back cover. Amazon's Cover Creator makes it easy to turn your ebook cover into a paperback cover. It formats your your cover and sizes it to match your chosen book size. You'll need to add the same cover artwork, spine title and write the back page copy.

The primary job of your book cover is to get the reader's attention, so they click over to your description to learn more. For a successful cover design, make sure it includes these essential elements:

Bright, contrasting colors - make your cover "pop" so that it stands out to browsing shoppers.   Good color combinations are:

- Orange/Teal
- Black/Gray/Red
- Purple/Yellow

When determining the colors for your book cover, take a look at the color schemes of successful books in your genre. You want to make sure your book matches what readers expect to see when searching around that topic. Research what is popular in your category. Look at the bestselling books and notice what colors they're using. Also pay attention to the contrasting colors and the combinations of light and dark colors. Make sure you have enough contrast to make your cover impactful and a good balance of light and dark, so that it looks professional.

Simple image - Nonfiction books do not need elaborate illustrations or images. They can stand out with bright colors and simple images. Large text alone is also effective. Simplicity is key. Choose an image that will mean something to the reader and illustrates how your book solves their problem. Canva provides images you can use for free, or there are several websites that offer free stock images One of my favorite sites for free images is **unsplash.com**.

Plenty of Space - Most non-fiction books have a central background color or gradient, and a simple image that illustrates a concept. The default spacing between letters is usually too cramped for a book cover, so add more space between the letters of the text. This is especially true for the author name.

Juxtaposition - Non-fiction books appeal to the brain. Catch the brain's attention by showing a juxtaposition – unexpected things that shouldn't really go together. A central "gimmick" with a solid color background - orange and yellow are popular colors for business books. Look at the bestselling books in your category and design yours in a similar way.

Balanced Text - The wrong font choice can make your book look unprofessional. A serif mixed with a sans-serif font make a nice contrast. Use only one bold or unique font on the title, and a simple font on the subtitle and your name. Try to fit the words together in a balanced way. Small words like "the, in, of, and, by…" can be italicized, lower case, and made small to fit between larger text.

What To Include On The Back Cover

While you'll only create a back cover for your paperback version, readers will see the back cover of a print book on your Amazon product page. In fact, almost everyone reads the blurb on the back of the book before they decide to buy. What's more, they only spend about 10 seconds doing it. Your back cover should make shoppers impatient to find out what's inside your book. Don't overcrowd your back cover. Allow for blank space and be selective on the text you place on the back cover. The back cover is essentially a compact version of your Amazon description. The most effective back covers include:

Tagline

Grab a reader's attention the moment they flip it over. The tagline can be a short descriptive sentence. a catchphrase or a quote from the book.

Blurb

A back blurb is your 10-second elevator pitch when readers look at your book. The secret to a great blurb is to know your audience. Write it with the reader's desires in mind. Present the problem. Promise answers. Say exactly what they'll take away from the book.

Author Bio

The bio on the back cover is more concise than any of your other "About the Author" descriptions. You must include an author bio on the back cover copy to convince readers of your authority, but you have limited space, so keep it brief and clear.

Testimonials

The back of a book cover is the perfect place to put social proof. Testimonials are a persuasive way to transform shoppers into readers.

"Start writing, no matter what. The water does not flow until the faucet is turned on."

— Louis L'Amour

Chapter 10: Publish & Promote

Now that you've completed all the hard work of writing and publishing your book, you need to make sure people see it. Fortunately, there are many book marketing options available that won't break the bank, and I'm going to share what's worked for me. Provided you've done the right research and selected a topic that has demand, these techniques should work well for you too. Remember, if you have too limited of an audience, no amount of promotion will keep it ranked high. However, if the purpose of your book is to build credibility and authority on your topic, then rankings are not your primary concern. If you've provided a quality resource on the subject, you'll enjoy some book sales and build your brand.

Set Up A Pre-Release

As we discussed in Chapter 8, pre-orders are a great way to promote your book when you have an existing audience or email list. When you set up the ability for pre-orders, you can gain early sales that help improve your ranking when you officially release your book. You can announce your upcoming book by sending an email to your list or post it on social media. Let them know you're looking for some volunteers to read it for free and give your a book a review on the release day.

Set Up A Free KDP Promotion

Once your book is live you can set up your first KDP Free Book promotion on Amazon. This is a great way to launch your book and get it in the hands of as many readers as possible. While it's free, send the link to some close friends and ask them to give your book a review. When they download the free version, it still counts as a verified purchase. Note: Don't ask family members to submit an official review your book, especially those who share your last name. Amazon is smart and is able to detect when someone is too close to you and will reject it as a verified review. However, you can include any of their reviews in the Editorial Review section. You can participate in a Kindle Free Book Promotion for a maximum of five days. In order to get the greatest sales impact from the giveaway, get the word out to book blogs and sites that aggregate freebies from around the web. I've used Freebooksy, Free Kindle Books and Tips, and Bookbub.

You'll also want to get the word out among your own connections. Announce your free book promotion through your own social media channels and by email.

Set Up a 99 Cent Promotion

After your free promotion and you have at least 10 reviews, set your price at 99 cents and promote it on BuckBooks. During the promotion, email your list about the promotion and post it on your social media accounts. To maximize your rankings, leave your price set at 99 cents for three to five days.

Develop A Relationship With Your Readers

In the front and back of your book, offer a free resource in exchange for their email address. By building an audience list, you can let them know when you release other books and ask them for reviews. Your free resource should be a link to something your readers will want. When they click on the link, it takes them to a place to subscribe to your list and download the free resource.

Collect Editorial Reviews

Order author copies of your paperback book and send them to your personal network. Then you can ask for a review to copy and paste into the editorial review area of your listing. The author price for your own books is the printing cost. You'll pay tax and shipping charges for each order. Here's how to order author copies:

1. Go to your Bookshelf and select the paperback you'd like to order.
2. Click Order Author Copies link in the yellow box ("...") menu to the right of your book title.
3. Enter quantity and choose the Amazon marketplace closest to your shipping destination.
4. Click Proceed to checkout to complete your order.

Set Up Your Amazon Author Page

It's very simple to create an Author Page that will help turn potential readers into lifelong fans. This is your personal feature page on Amazon. Many authors overlook setting up an account on Amazon Author Central. On your Author Page, people can learn more about you, see all of your books, find your website, blog, or social media all in one spot on Amazon. It also gives you the ability to:

- Fill in the Editorial Reviews section for your book
- Track your Book Sales
- Respond to Reviews
- Improve your discoverability in search engines such as Google
- Connect with readers through additional content such as your Twitter feed, blog posts, videos and photos

To take advantage of creating your Author Page, you'll need to sign up for an Author Central Amazon account. To make a professional author page, include the following:

- Compelling Biography
- Professional Author Photo
- All of Your Books
- Promotional Videos
- Feed to Your Blog Posts
- Social Media and Website Information

How to set up your Author Central Account:

- Go to https://authorcentral.amazon.com/ and select "Join Now"

- Sign in with your regular Amazon username and password. If you don't have an account, select I am a new customer. You'll need to give a little more information.

- Read the Terms and Conditions then click Accept.

- Enter the name your books are written under. A list of possible books appears.

- Select any one of your books to create the account.

- If your book is not in the list, you can search for it by title or ISBN. Your book must be available for purchase on Amazon in order to setup an Author Central Amazon Account.

- Amazon will send you a confirmation email to finish creating the account.

While you're waiting for verification, you can start adding information to your Author Page. You cannot add or make changes to your books or blog until your identity is confirmed, but don't let that stop you from getting started.

You can start adding things like pictures and a bio right away.

Complete Your Author Page:

Tell potential readers about yourself. Your author bio should include keywords you want connected to you and your books. Consider adding interesting facts about your background, awards, hobbies, projects — anything that legitimatizes you as an author and connects you with readers. Mention where people can find you on your website, blog or social media. Show potential readers who you are as a person.

Add Photos

Some authors include one professional headshot, while others include a variety of professional and personal pictures. For example, you might add a picture of your family, a picture of you speaking if you're a professional speaker, or a picture of you showing a house if you're a realtor.

Add Your Blog Feed

You can show teasers of your latest blog feeds by linking your blog to your Page on Author Central. That way, when you add a post to your blog, it will automatically show in the blog feed on your Author page. This can increase traffic to your blog and keep readers connected to you. For complete instructions, follow Amazon's instructions on Author Central.

Add Video

Having a book video or author video will really personalize and enhance your Author Page. You can upload up to eight videos, less than 10 minutes long and choose the order they appear on your page.

Add Your Books

On the Author Central Books tab, scroll to the bottom of your bibliography and click Add more books. In the search bar, type your author name, book title, or ISBN, and click Go. Once you've found the title, click "This is my book" below the book. Amazon should list your name as the author.

If you're not listed as the author, or your book is not appearing, you'll need to troubleshoot with Amazon on their Help pages.

Add Editorial Reviews

Including an editorial review for your book is a great addition to your Amazon book sales page — yet many authors don't take advantage of it. The editorial review section, located on your book's sales page, allows you to list reviews, comments, or testimonials that others have said about you, your book, or your previous books. You can also use this area to feature your top five reviews of your book to maximize their exposure. Here's how to add editorial reviews:

- Click the Books tab at the top of the page.
- Click on the book you want and select the correct edition.
- Under Editorial Reviews, click Add.
- Follow the instructions to enter the review, the name of who wrote the review, and the name of the publication, website, or how the review was received.

"All you have to do is write one true sentence. Write the truest sentence that you know."

— Ernest Hemingway

Chapter 11: Amazon Advertising

Amazon Marketing Services (AMS) allows authors to advertise their books in Amazon search results and on the sales pages of other books. This is an effective way to leverage the millions of customers shopping for books on Amazon. It also lets you choose where and how people find your book. You can put your book in front of people who are looking to buy their next book - which is not true for Google Ads or Facebook Ads. What's even better, you can name your own price for each click, and you don't pay until someone clicks your ad.

Your First Amazon Ad Campaign

Before you can create an ad campaign, you need to first set up your **Amazon Marketing Services Account.** Go to your KDP Bookshelf. Next to your published book click the button that says "Promote and Advertise." On the following screen, click on the yellow button that reads, "Create an Ad Campaign." You'll then be directed to set up your AMS account. Select "I have a Kindle Direct

Publishing Account." After clicking "Next Step, your KDP account should be linked to your AMS account.

The AMS Dashboard

When you set up your first ad campaign, you'll see the AMS Dashboard. This is where you'll manage and track your campaigns.

Campaign Name: Important when running several campaigns. Tip: use an abbreviated name of the book, a detail about the campaign, and the date. This format will help you monitor and manage your ads easily.

Status: Delivering, Paused, Suspended, Pending Review. To pause a campaign, click on the drop down menu.

Type: Sponsored Product (SP) or Lockscreen Ad (LA)

- **Sponsored Product** ads promote your book to shoppers actively searching with related keywords or viewing similar products on Amazon.
- **Lockscreen Ads** are based on shoppers' interests and are shown when the unlock their Kindle E-readers or Fire Tablets to begin reading or shopping for books.

They are pay-per-click, interest-targeted display ads that appear on Kindle E-reader and Fire Tablet lockscreens and home screens. Lockscreen Ads reach customers on their devices, where they are reading and making ebook purchasing decisions. Ads are targeted by genre interests.

Start Date, End Date: If your campaign is running continuously, you'll see a dash under End Date.

Budget: You'll set a daily budget or total budget

Spend: The total amount of money you've spent on that campaign

Orders: The number of orders from Amazon shoppers after clicking on your ads.

Sales: The total value of products sold from clicking on your ads.

ACoS: This stands for Advertising Cost of Sales. It is the average amount spent on the campaign/divided by the total sales. This tells you if your campaign is profitable.

The lower the percentage, the more profitable the campaign.

To take into account Amazon's cut of your book sales in your profitability, use this rule of thumb:

If your Kindle book is priced from 2.99 - 9.99, you need an ACoS of 70% or lower to break even.

If your Kindle book is priced less than 2.99 or greater than 9.99, you need an ACoS of 35% or lower to break even.

The following terms appear on the very top of the AMS Dashboard:

Spend: The total amount of money you've spent on that campaign

Sales: The total value of products sold from clicking on your ads.

ACoS: Advertising Cost of Sales — the average amount spent on the campaign/divided by the total sales.

Impressions: The total number of times your ad was shown on an Amazon page.

Clicks: The average number of times someone clicked on your ads. Remember, you only pay for ads when someone clicks on it.

CPC: The average cost per click.

CTR: The average clickthrough rate

Sales: All sales made from someone clicking on your ad within the specified time frame. KDP sales reports show the final numbers, so they may be different from what you see here. Note: It takes about two days for sales to reflect in the total. You'll see the click, the spend - but the sale won't be updated for about two days.

Research AMS Keywords

AMS Keywords are the words you want your book to show up for when a shopper types them into Amazon. Your book will then show up for that particular search result.

Tips for choosing keywords:

- **Don't choose keywords that no one is searching for**. It's important to choose keywords that shoppers actually use. If no one ever types your keywords into

Amazon, then there will be no opportunity for Amazon to show your ad.

- **Don't choose keywords that are too competitive**. Search terms that are too competitive will also cause problems. If thousands of people type your term into Amazon every day, you'll be competing with hundreds of big time publishers and merchandisers for that term. This will make your Cost Per Click very high. It is also unlikely that your ad will show up.

- **Choose plenty of keywords**. If you select only a directly correlated keywords, you likely won't get enough impressions for a profitable campaign. Often, some of the most profitable keywords are something that aren't directly related to your book. It takes experimentation to discover the most profitable keywords. Set a goal of finding 200 to 300 AMS keywords.

- **Understand the difference between KDP keywords and AMS keywords.** When setting up your listing you chose KDP keywords. Amazon does not allow you to target other books when selecting KDP keywords. With AMS keywords you are allowed to target other successful books using the title and the author name. This is an effective strategy.

Your keywords need to be words that people would type into the Search box. They can be:

- **Descriptive phrases** - words that people use to describe a book or topic they're searching. This could be a description of their need, or how they would describe it if they don't already have a specific book they're searching for.
- **Related book titles and authors** - names of books and authors related to your book

Build Your AMS Keyword List

You'll want to create a list of words that your target market would type into Amazon if they were looking for your type of book. Use a spreadsheet to organize your list. Start by brainstorming any words that come to mind when describing your book. While in incognito mode, type these words into the Amazon search bar to see other suggested terms. (Remember, incognito mode prevents Amazon from using your account information or previous searches when showing you suggestions.) Make sure you select "Kindle Store" in Amazon so the suggestions will be focused on books. Just as we did when selecting KDP keywords, type the phrases, and Amazon will show you suggestions. Write down those words that are a good fit for your book.

Just as we did before, type one of your terms followed by an "A" and see what Amazon suggests. Then type "B," and so on through the alphabet. Write down the terms that are a good fit. Try to find at least 50 keywords using this method. Repeat the steps and see what else you can come up with until you have 50 words on your list.

Next, start adding keywords related to other book titles and authors. Here's how: Type your best descriptive terms into Amazon and click search. Amazon presents a list of books. Add each book title and author name to your list. Click on the books you think best represent your book. Copy the titles and author names that appear in the "Customers who bought this item also bought" section. Next, click on the related categories to see the top 20 books in that category. Add the title and author names of these books to your list. Go to the next page and copy the information on the books that rank 21-40. To the right of the top books in each category are the "Hot New Releases." Click on this and copy the title and author names of the top 20 books here as well. Because they are new, they don't have much competition in AMS yet, and they're in a big launch period. This means they have a high number of impressions and low competition. Repeat the steps until you have at least 200 keywords on your list.

KDP Rocket is a paid tool that does all of this work for you. If you have the budget, it will save you a lot of time. They also have a free AMS course that is very worthwhile.

How To Set Up A Sponsored Product Ad

1. Go into your KDP account and find the book you want to advertise. Select "Promote and Advertise."
2. Click on "Create an Ad Campaign."
3. Re-log into your KDP Account then select "Sponsored Products Ad."
4. A list of your published books will appear. Select the book you're creating the campaign for.
5. Scroll down and give your campaign a name. Tip: You can name your campaign an abbreviated name of your

book, a detail about the campaign, and the date. That way when you have many ads, this format will help you monitor and manage your ads more easily.

6. Set the duration. You can run your campaign without an end date or set a specific date range. Amazon recommends running campaigns for a minimum of two weeks to make sure they get traction.

7. Set your daily budget. This is the maximum amount you're willing to spend per day on this campaign. The minimum daily budget is $1, and you'll only be charged when a customer clicks your ad. The daily budget is an average over the duration of your campaign. That means some days may exceed your daily budget, while other days won't. At the end of the campaign, the average daily spend won't exceed your daily budget.

8. You can choose from two types of targeting: **Manual Targeting** allows you to target by product to reach readers as they browse detail pages similar to yours. Manual Targeting also allows you to target by keyword and add your own keywords based on your book's content, genre, and similar authors. You can also use suggested keywords provided when you're creating your campaign. Amazon recommends a minimum of

100 keywords for each campaign. With **Automatic Targeting**, Amazon will choose keywords that it perceives to closely align with your book topic. This is a great starting point if you don't know which targeting type to use. With some effort in finding the right keywords, Manual Targeting can be more profitable. We will cover how to do this below.

9. Choose an Ad format: Choose from **Custom** where you'll include your own ad copy to provide readers with context for your book. **Standard** allows you to launch a campaign quickly without custom text.

10. Select the book you want to set up the ad for.

11. If you selected Manual Targeting above, you'll choose either **Keyword Targeting** or **Product Targeting**. Use the keyword targeting strategy when you know the search terms that customers use to search products similar to yours. With product targeting, you'll choose specific products, categories, brands, or other product features to target your ads. Use this strategy to help shoppers find your product when browsing detail pages and categories or searching products on Amazon.

12. Set Default Cost Per Click (CPC bid). All your keywords in this campaign will start with this CPC. You can always change this after your ad goes live.

13. Click on "Suggested Keywords" to add keywords Amazon thinks pertain to your book.

14. Click on "Enter Keywords" to manually add words or phrases. You also have the option to upload a file to add a large volume of keywords.

15. Click "Add" and you'll see your added keywords and their CPC under Added Keywords.

16. Write your Ad Text under "Creative"

17. Think of your ad text as your elevator pitch. It cannot be greater than 150 characters.

18. Add payment information. If you don't already have a credit card attached to your account, then you'll need to add a payment method.

19. You can choose to "Save as Draft" if you're not ready to finalize your ad, or "Launch Campaign."

20. You'll get an email from Amazon saying your campaign is under review. It usually takes 1-3 days, then once approved your campaign will be live. If you receive a message saying it was rejected, they will inform you of any text that needs to be changed.

How To Set Up A Lockscreen Ad

1. Follow steps 1-5 above, selecting "Lockscreen Ads."

2. Select the book you want to create the ad for.

3. Choose interests for your campaign.

4. Amazon will show your ad based on these interests associated with your book.

5. Give your campaign a name using the same format.

6. Set a Cost Per Click bid.

7. Set your Campaign Budget. This is the total amount your willing to spend for the duration of your campaign. The minimum budget is $100.

8. Select the start and end dates for your campaign.

9. Select the Pacing for your campaign. You can choose to run the campaign as quickly as possible, or spread the campaign evenly over its duration.

10. Complete Your Headline and Text copy. The headline allows for only 50 characters, while the text section allows for 150 characters.

11. Preview your ad in the different dimensions.

12. When you're ready, click "Submit Campaign for Review." It will take 1-3 days before Amazon will get notify your approval or rejection of the ad.

Analyze & Adjust Your Ad Campaigns

The best results come from continuous monitoring, optimizing, and general upkeep of your campaigns after they're setup. After weeks of working with the system, many authors find opportunities that weren't obvious when they first started. Consistently monitor and make changes to your campaigns to generate traffic to your books. Check your campaigns at least three times a week. If you're first campaign doesn't bring you a return, use what you learn from that campaign and keep adjusting until you have a profitable campaign.

Allow your AMS campaigns to run for at least 7 days before making changes. This will allow enough time for AMS to show enough data for you to make the right decisions on optimizing your campaigns. Keep in mind, Amazon does not show your ad history with specific date ranges. You can only see the overall history of your campaign. If you want to track it by date range, you'll want to build your own tracking spreadsheet by exporting the data each time you check it.

To increase your ad's profitability, you can adjust your bid and CPC (cost-per-click) to get your ad in front of more shoppers. Sometimes, even a minor change such as increasing your CPC bid just 15 cents can lead to positive results. You'll need to test and change your CPC bid to see what causes positive results for your campaign.

Tip: If one of your keywords is getting a lot of impressions and then it stops, try increasing your CPC bid. If you think a specific keyword is perfect for advertising but you aren't getting enough impressions, or you think your CPC bid is too high, try adding that keyword to your listing description where it fits naturally - to your title, subtitle, book description, or inside the book itself. This will increase your book's relevance.

If your ads aren't performing the way you expected, there are a few things to check to make sure your ads have the best chance possible of succeeding:

Campaign Pacing - If you selected "spread campaign evenly over its duration" or if the budget looks like it could run out by the end of the campaign (based on the predicted amount of clicks and cost-per-click), the budget will be spread evenly, but performance may be sporadic. This means the ad may not show to everyone who's viewing relevant pages, because the campaign must continue serving ads until the last day.

Relevance - The more customers click on an ad, the more relevant it becomes. The less related your book is to your targeting, the less likely your ad will perform. Make sure your targeting is relevant to your title because once the auction market has enough competition, better-performing ads will push out less relevant ones.

Targeting - Too few keywords, products, or interests may limit the reach of the campaign to a smaller audience. You can add up to 1,000 keywords or products and as many interests as you want. Amazon recommends targeting at least 100 keywords to get started.

Duration - If your campaign is too short, it may not run to full potential. Amazon recommends setting Sponsored Products campaigns for a minimum of two weeks. You can run your campaign with no end date and terminate or pause it at any time. Keep in mind that ads may still run for 24 hours after you have terminated or paused them, so you may continue to accrue impressions, clicks, charges and sales for 14 days. Remember to match your duration with the right budget. Too small of a budget may impact the ad campaign performance.

Bids - If your cost-per-click bid is lower than existing live ads, your ad may not be shown. Look for the suggested bid range in the campaign builder and keep within those parameters. You will only be charged when a customer clicks your ad.

"You can make anything by writing."

— C.S. Lewis

Thank you!

Thanks for purchasing my book and welcome to the world of self-publishing. I encourage you to make the most of the opportunities that can come with it. So unlock the possibilities! What's next for you? Speaking engagements? An online course? Another book? I look forward to hearing about it!

You may also like **The Guided Writer Self-Publishing Course.** Based on feedback from my readers, I've learned many people like the idea of having someone to coach them through the writing and publishing process. In this action-oriented course, I guide you through the process, step-by-step, of writing and self-publishing your book from start-to finish.

The Guided Writer course includes:

- Four Learning Modules
- 20 Video Lessons
- 67 Page Digital Workbook

I hope to see you there.

Sign up for my course:

Get Published
Guided Writer
C o u r s e

guidedwritercourse.writerrs.com

Remember, if you enjoyed the book, I would love it if you would **post a review** on Amazon. As my thank you, I'm giving you my template for creating opt-in freebie ebooks ($19 value). In this ready to use PowerPoint file, you get a pre-designed layout with a writing formula that converts. You'll save time on tedious page layout/design and eliminate the guesswork. Simply customize the template and save it as a PDF to use in your sales funnel.

To access your free ebook creator template, visit:

writerrs.com/product/e-book-template/

Enter the coupon code: FREEBIE

If you'd like to check out my other titles, I'll tell you about each book on the next few pages.

If you have questions that I haven't answered, be sure to contact me at **writerrs.com**, and I'll get right back to you. Here's to your success!

Online Learning and Course Design Book

The Step-By-Step Guide to Copywriting: Online Learning and Course Design: Share Your Knowledge, Teach and Make Money Online (Copywriter's Toolbox Book 1)

Available on Amazon

You've written your book. Now turn it into a course.

This book walks you through every step of creating an effective online learning course using time-tested principles of instructional design and instructional writing. It's a multi-step guide that subject matter experts and copywriters can follow to go from idea to fully developed online course. Whether your course will be sold on a marketplace platform such as Udemy, self-hosted on your own website, or launched through sites such as Teachable, Thinkific, or Kajabi, this book will help you - even if you're not sure yet on what type of course you want to create.

Turn your expertise into passive income

- Take advantage of the surge in popularity E-learning has seen over the last few years.
- Create engaging materials so that your audience gains and retains the knowledge and skills you're teaching.
- Design your course according to how adults actually learn.
- Learn how to evaluate the effectiveness your course.
- Make sure your course isn't boring!

Are you interested in creating and selling your own e-course? This book is for you if you're interested in creating and selling your own online training course that facilitates true change for your students. It's not a get rich quick scheme, but a reference on how to design a quality course that your students will be happy they purchased - bringing you rave reviews and increasing your credibility in your field.

Are you a freelance copywriter? The popularity of online learning has created a new opportunity for copywriters. This book will help you create courses for your clients.

Are you a subject matter expert or solopreneur?
Do you think of yourself as a subject matter authority? If you have experience in a subject area, chances are you're further along on that journey than many other people. You may have expertise in a certain type of business, or you may have mastered a skill that others may want to learn. Leverage your knowledge to increase your income with a well-written course. Whatever the subject, the eLearning industry is an enormous, modern-day opportunity to make money online, leverage your knowledge and generate passive income in an entirely new way.

Become an authority.
If you're in business, your own online course can help you get your message out to the market and establish you as an authority in your industry. If you have a special talent or

skill, you can share it with the world. Even better - you can create a passive income stream in the process. If you have mastery or knowledge of a subject, you can teach it!

Learn Instructional Design Best Practices From a Professional If your courses create true change for your students, then you're well on your way to success in the online training world. I wrote this book to help you do just that. As a professional copywriter and instructional designer, I've created corporate training courses in a variety of formats over the past twenty-five years. I'm sharing my extensive real-world experience in course writing and design, along with time-tested instructional design principles. Put this practical advice and tips to work for you to create quality content. The Step-By-Step Guide to Copywriting: Online Learning and Course Design is perfect for professionals, business owners, bloggers, or anyone interested in creating an online course for content marketing purposes. Freelance writers who have never written training courses can use this book as a guide to providing an additional writing service for their clients.

What Is Content Strategy?

What Is Content Strategy? A Beginner's Guide for Standing Out Online (Content Marketing for Beginners Book 2)

Available on Amazon

Do you want to write content that builds your audience?

If you don't have millions to spend on a big marketing campaign, you need to create great content to gain traffic and sell your products. But how do you do this if you're not a content marketing expert? You need a plan to follow and a way to organize your plan.

Exact instructions to organize your content writing. This book is your framework to plan and create endless, powerful content for your blog or business.Put your content plan into action.This system can be used for both digital or paper journals.

Get more shares. Write content that your customers will want to read and share. Create content with purpose and passion.

Get more traffic. Learn how to provide value to your audience and maximize your traffic. Write strategic content that builds your business.

Boost your sales. Implement a content marketing plan that will drive traffic and increase your sales. Create a content strategy for your blog or business.

You can write great content that creates great customers! Just follow this formula to learn how to do it.

The One Year Content Strategy Workbook for Entrepreneurs

The One Year Content Strategy Workbook for Entrepreneurs: A Digital Marketing Journal Planner and Editorial Blog Calendar (Content Marketing for Beginners)

Available on Amazon

The companion planner to *What Is Content Strategy?* This pre-designed planner is set-up with fill-in-the-blank pages using the systems described in the book. Use the planner to organize your content writing for your blog or business.

Put your content plan into action. It's your framework to plan and create endless, powerful content for your blog or business. Implement content marketing habits that will boost your sales.

Create content with purpose and passion. Write content that your customers will want to read and share.

Build your business. Learn how to provide value to your audience and maximize your traffic. Write strategic content that builds your business. Inside this book you'll find:

- Fill-in-the-blank pages to create your content strategy
- A format and prompts to plan your content for your blog or business
- A planner to create your Monthly Editorial Calendar and Daily Logs

Freelance Writing Book

The Mighty Writer Field Guide: Set Up A Freelance Writing Business in Five Days: Make Money From Home With Templates and Proven Systems To Become A Writer That Thrives Instead of Survives (Copywriter's Toolbox Book 4)

Available on Amazon

Yes, it is possible to thrive as a well-paid freelance writer instead of bidding on low paying jobs, or writing on spec. From my own experience, I spell out exactly how to start making money quickly by starting your own freelance business from scratch. Learn the exact tactics I have used to earn as much as $95 per hour, with nothing more than a computer and internet connection. It takes very little money to start, and you don't need prior experience. Plus, you can get up and running quickly so you can make money right away. It's not a get-rich-quick scheme, but a realistic guide for becoming a consistently paid freelance writer. In this book I simplify the hype and bust the myths of the starving writer by answering the most pressing questions: How do I find clients?How can I break into freelance writing if I have no experience?How can I get paid well as a writer? With the book, you'll receive my copy/paste templates and worksheets in *The Business Startup Kit for Writers* for FREE with the purchase of this book ($25 value). For 5 days, you'll complete a set of To-Do List items for each day. By the end of 5 days, you'll be ready to get started making money from home as freelance writer. *The Mighty Writers Field Guide* will teach you a simple system for building income that allows you to:

• Work where you want and when you want.
• Set your own hours and build a business of your own.

- Earn as much or as little as you want, depending on how much time you put into it.
- Choose the type of projects to work on and exactly what hours you want to work from anywhere in the world.
- Get paid well, rather than earning pennies per word.

In today's gig economy, the opportunities for freelance writers are endless. Whether you want to start a side hustle to supplement your income, or run a full-time business, you can get started making money from home as a freelance writer - and getting paid well - to write in the business world. You'll learn real ways to find clients and get paid well to write, not apply for low-paying job postings that go to the lowest bidder. If you like to write - and want to make money doing it - this book will show you how to do it quickly!

Airbnb Hosting Guide

Airbnb Toolbox: How To Fuel Your Airbnb Listing to Work For You: A Workbook for Hosts: Includes Tips, Worksheets, Checklists & Templates (Airbnb Host How To Guides)

Available on Amazon

Airbnb for Smart Hosts (Not Airbnb For Dummies)

The Airbnb Toolbox™ puts your Airbnb listing to work for you. Whether you are a new Airbnb Host, or you're looking to take your vacation rental business to the next level, my Perfect Host System™ will make the difference between average guest reviews and 5-star reviews. As a profitable Airbnb Host since 2013, I've compiled everything I've learned along the way that will save you time and avoid the costly mistakes of learning by trial and error. Whether it's a real estate rental property or a spare room, this will set you up for success. You'll get checklists, cheat sheets, and copy/paste templates to make it happen.

Learn Airbnb Secrets for Success With Practical Tips, Worksheets+Templates Get exclusive access to my private Library of Templates. Download copy/paste files such as messages I send to my guests, my rental contract, House Manual template, Supplies Checklist + other secrets that have helped me run my successful Airbnb business.

Maximize your bookings, increase your Airbnb listing rank, and reduce the amount of time you spend managing your Airbnb business. I share easy ways that I use to build

5 Star Reviews and simple ways to solve common host problems. With the popularity of Airbnb, there is a lot of competition. That means you must succeed at getting your property in the mind's eye of travelers, or they'll move on to the next one. After your quality photos, your listing title and description must tell and sell. This workbook walks you through a specific way to write your profile, title, and description. When you're finished, you'll have a completed listing description that will set you up for success. You'll learn about:

- How to win over travelers through an engaging profile and an inspiring listing description.
- Establishing House Rules.
- Determining your nightly rate to maximize your profit.
- How to optimize your listing on Airbnb.
- Staging and preparing your space.
- Enhancing your guests' experience.
- Writing a Welcome Book.
- Greeting your guests.
- Saying goodbye to your guests.
- How to generate predictable positive reviews.
- Efficient housecleaning and changeover recommendations.

- Managing your schedule to maximize time.
- Identifying people to assist you.

What's Your Time Worth to You?

The Perfect Host System™, provides strategies to manage your time and put your real estate investment to work for you, instead of trading your time for money. It puts it on autopilot so you stay organized and ahead of everyday tasks.

Become a Five Star Airbnb Host

Learn simple strategies to help manage guest reviews and minimize negative reviews.

If you're a new Airbnb Host, this guide is for you.

Airbnb Host Tax Planning Guide

Airbnb Host Tax Planning and Bookkeeping Guide: How to Keep Financial Records for Your Vacation Rental

Available on Amazon

Airbnb hosts get your finances organized and save money at tax time. If you haven't been tracking your expenses or keeping complete records for your Airbnb business, you may be leaving money on the table. While many of us would rather leave the accounting to the professionals, it doesn't hurt to know the basics so that we know how to keep accurate records and take advantage of valuable tax deductions. That's why I've assembled some basic information you need to know into this guide - to save you time in researching answers to common questions and to give you simple tips and strategies to stay financially organized with your Airbnb rental.

The Author Effect

Sandra Shillington is a five time Amazon bestselling author and has been writing for large and small businesses since 1988. She loves nothing more than absorbing new information and transforming it into engaging copy. After self-publishing her first book in 2010, Sandra and has been an ardent learner of all things Kindle Direct Publishing. She stays well-versed on the latest knowledge of Amazon self-publishing and strives to learn everything she can about building a portfolio of self-published books while helping others do the same. While earning her Bachelor's degree in Business at Pepperdine University, she could not ignore her passion for writing. In the midst of economics, finance, and accounting, she also studied public relations, business writing, and creative nonfiction writing. After college, she worked in the corporate world as an Instructional Designer, writing and designing training courses. She eventually left the 9 to 5 routine and went on to write advertising copy, web content, articles and courses for both large and small companies — leading her to start Writerrs.com.

Join the Mighty Online Creators Community

If you want to stay on top of the latest advice on designing and building courses, writing and publishing books, and creating audio, video and written assets for your business, Join my Facebook Group, Mighty Online Creators. It's for entrepreneurs, business owners and professionals who want to make a bigger impact (and more income) by:

• Creating an online course

• Self-publishing a book

• Writing a blog

• Starting a podcast or YouTube Channel

• Launching a freelance career

Join Mighty Online Creators at:

facebook.com/groups/MightyOnlineCreators/

Also, sign up to receive your free

Faster Writing Cheat Sheet:

fasterwritingcheatsheet.writerrs.com

www.ingramcontent.com/pod-product-compliance
Lightning Source LLC
Chambersburg PA
CBHW072132280526
45788CB00002B/607